LA SALLE

Early Texas Explorer

Stephanie Kuligowski, M.A.T.

Consultant

Devia Cearlock
K–12 Social Studies Specialist
Amarillo Independent School District

Publishing Credits

Dona Herweck Rice, *Editor-in-Chief*
Lee Aucoin, *Creative Director*
Marcus McArthur, Ph.D., *Associate Education Editor*
Neri Garcia, *Senior Designer*
Stephanie Reid, *Photo Editor*
Rachelle Cracchiolo, M.S.Ed., *Publisher*

Image Credits:

Cover Newscom & Getty Images; p.1 Getty Images;
pp.4–5 The Granger Collection; p.5 (sidebar) LOC
[LC–USZ62–3329]; p.6 Lycée Corneille, Rouen;
p.7 The Granger Collection; p.7 (sidebar) Bridgeman
Art Library; p.9 (top) Getty Images; p.9 (bottom)
Getty Images; p.8 North Wind Picture Archives;
p.9 LOC [LC–USZ62–45558]; p.10 North Wind Picture
Archives; p.11 North Wind Picture Archives; p.12 (top)
North Wind Picture Archives; p.12 (bottom) Alamy;
p.13 Alamy; pp.2–3, 14 North Wind Picture Archives;
p.15 North Wind Picture; p.16 Bridgeman Art Library;
p.17 (top) LOC [LC–D4–22686]; p.17 (bottom) LOC
[LC–USZ62–90556]; p.17 (sidebar) iStockphoto;
p.18 North Wind Picture Archives; p.19 Associated
Press; p.20 The Granger Collection; p.21 Illinois
Historical State Library; p.22 Associated Press;
p.23 Louis XIV Collection; p.24 Bridgeman Art
Library; p.25 North Wind Picture Archives; p.26 The
Granger Collection; p.27 North Wind Picture Archives;
p.28 Timothy J. Bradley; p.29 Newscom; p.32 LOC
[LC–D4–22686]; All other images Shutterstock.

Teacher Created Materials

5301 Oceanus Drive
Huntington Beach, CA 92649-1030
http://www.tcmpub.com

ISBN 978-1-4333-5043-6
© 2013 Teacher Created Materials, Inc.

Table of Contents

Age of Discovery

René-Robert Cavelier (ruh-NEY roh-BEAR ka-vuh-LYEY), also known as Sieur de La Salle (sewr dyoo luh sahl), was born in 1643. This was an exciting time to live in Europe. The continent was in the midst of a cultural **revival**. Artists were painting and sculpting great works. Scientists were making new discoveries. And explorers were traveling to faraway lands.

La Salle grew up in Rouen (roo-AHN), France. Rouen was a port city on the Seine (seyn) River. Ships sailed past Rouen on their way to foreign lands across the Atlantic Ocean. More than 1,000 ships sailed in and out of Rouen each year.

As a boy growing up in a port town, La Salle saw many sailors from other countries. He heard tales of New World adventures. This "New World" was North America. People were already living in North America. But this land was new to Europeans. Spain, England, and France had all claimed land there. The French had started New France in modern-day Canada.

La Salle dreamed of New France as a child. He imagined a future full of adventure and discovery.

Samuel de Champlain

Real Life Heroes

As a boy, La Salle heard about the adventures of French explorers in the New World. These explorers, such as Samuel de Champlain (SAM-yoo-el day sham-PLEYN) and Jacques Cartier (zhahk KAR-tee-ay), became the young boy's heroes.

Name Change

La Salle had a privileged childhood. His father, Jean Cavelier (zhan ka-vuh-LYEY), was a successful merchant in Rouen. The family owned several estates. One of them was called *La Salle*. The tradition in France was for a son to take the name of a family estate. That is how René-Robert Cavelier came to be known as Sieur de La Salle, or "gentleman from La Salle."

Rouen, France

Ready for Adventure
School Years

La Salle was born into a wealthy French family. This meant that he could attend the best schools in France. These were **Jesuit** (JEZH-oo-it) schools. The Jesuits were an order, or group, of educated Catholic (KATH-uh-lik) priests. They ran schools and worked as **missionaries**. Missionaries are people who teach their religious beliefs to others.

Jesuit schools were not easy. The school day went from sunrise to sundown. Students studied the Bible and other subjects. Many students learned seven languages—French, Hebrew, Greek, Latin, Arabic, Spanish, and Italian.

La Salle's childhood school

Jesuit missionary in New France

Ignatius of Loyola

La Salle was a bright student. He wanted to know more about the places explorers were visiting. And he wanted to see them for himself.

At age 17, La Salle decided to become a priest. Most think he was lured by the promise of world travel. Catholic priests were being sent around the world to spread Christianity. La Salle's older brother, Jean, was also a priest. He had been sent to New France to do missionary work. In 1667, La Salle followed in his footsteps.

A missionary preaches to fur traders and American Indians.

Rugged Wilderness

La Salle arrived in New France and found his brother, Jean, who was a missionary in Montreal. Montreal was a small French **outpost** located on an island on the Saint Lawrence River. The land had long been home to many American Indian tribes. The French claimed the land. They built a mission, a hospital, and a **seminary** (SEM-uh-ner-ee). A seminary is a school that trains priests.

Montreal grew slowly because it had a **remote** location and faced many attacks by American Indians. It was the most dangerous place in New France. The priests sold land for low prices. They hoped that more French settlers would mean fewer American Indian attacks.

La Salle was granted a plot of land near the site now called the Lachine (luh-SHEEN) Rapids. He began clearing it for farming. His plan was to rent plots to farmers to pay for his travels. La Salle was different from the other settlers in Montreal. The priests wanted to convert natives to Christianity. The fur traders wanted to get rich. But La Salle craved adventure more than converts or riches.

map showing the plan for the Montreal outpost

A Dying Dream

In 1642, 21 people moved from France to Montreal Island. Their dream was to create an ideal Catholic community. They built a fort and named it *Ville-Marie*. But by the 1650s, constant attacks by American Indians had nearly ended their dream. They wanted more Europeans to settle there. So, they gave La Salle a large plot of land near the town.

Business Plan

La Salle needed money for his **expeditions**. Fur trading was the best business in New France. So La Salle set out to become a successful fur trader.

New World Success

La Salle wanted to be a good fur trader in New France. But he knew he had to befriend local American Indians. The locals were the best trappers. They knew where to find the animals whose **pelts** were in great demand. They traded pelts for cheap **trinkets**, guns, and alcohol. La Salle learned the languages of several friendly tribes. This helped him talk to the trappers.

American Indians sell beaver pelts to traders.

trading post

On his land, La Salle built a simple fort and a **trading post**. Its location made it easy for trappers to launch their canoes into the Saint Lawrence River. From there, they paddled into the wilderness. There they found many animals. La Salle paid trappers and traders for animal pelts. Soon, he had many men working for him. His business boomed.

La Salle heard about a major river that flowed to the sea. They called it the Ohio River. La Salle thought it led to the Gulf of California. But he was wrong. The French had been looking for a water route across North America to China. La Salle dreamed of making this important discovery for France.

Lachine

Many people in New France disliked La Salle. They made fun of his plan to reach China by water. They nicknamed his settlement near Montreal *La Chine*, which is French for China. Today it is called *Lachine*.

snowshoes

Wild Ways

In New France, La Salle learned wilderness survival skills quickly. In summer, he smeared himself with bear grease to keep mosquitoes away. In winter, he made snowshoes and wore them to explore the woods. He also wore American Indian **moccasins** and deerskin leggings on hikes into the woods.

The First Expedition
Dream Come True

La Salle

La Salle was eager to begin his first expedition. He sold his land to pay for supplies. He bought food, guns, and four large canoes. La Salle also hired 22 men and several Seneca (SEN-i-kuh) American Indian guides. A group of missionaries joined the group as well.

On July 6, 1669, the expedition left Montreal in search of a waterway to the ocean. They paddled up the Saint Lawrence River. Fallen trees and rocks often forced the men to carry their canoes overland. This was called *portaging* (POR-taj-ing). The journey was slow and difficult.

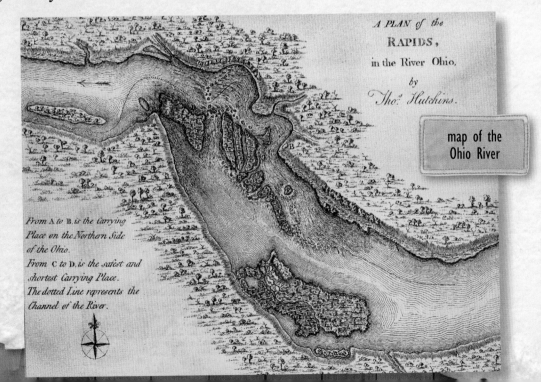

A PLAN of the RAPIDS, in the River Ohio, by Thoˢ Hutchins.

From A to B, is the Carrying Place on the Northern Side of the Ohio.
From C to D, is the safest and shortest Carrying Place.
The dotted Line represents the Channel of the River.

map of the Ohio River

American Indians travel by moonlight on the Ohio River.

In August, the group reached Lake Ontario. They paddled around the shore and met many friendly American Indians. One tribe gave La Salle a **captive** named Nika. Nika and La Salle became good friends. That winter, the men camped near the lake.

In the spring, the group reached the Ohio River. The river was full of boulders, **eddies**, and waterfalls. The frequent portaging made the trip miserable. There were also snakes and mosquitoes. The crew wanted to turn back, but La Salle refused.

Finally, a huge waterfall brought the expedition to a halt. One night, the crew snuck away, leaving La Salle and Nika alone in the wilderness.

Friends to the End

Nika was a Shawnee American Indian who had been taken prisoner by the Iroquois (IR-uh-kwoi). The Iroquois gave him to La Salle as a gift. La Salle and Nika quickly became friends. They learned each other's languages and had long talks as they hiked.

After their crew abandoned them, La Salle and Nika worked together to survive. They hunted, trapped, and **foraged** for food. In the winter of 1671, they made it safely back to Montreal. They would remain friends for the rest of their lives.

In a Position of Power

La Salle returned to Montreal. There he met the new governor of New France, Louis de Buade (LOO-ee day boo-AHD), Comte de Frontenac (KOHM-teh day FRAWN-tih-nak). He had the same dream as La Salle. Both men wanted to find a water route to the ocean.

In 1673, an expedition led by Frenchmen Jacques Marquette (mahr-KET) and Louis Joliet (joh-lee-ET) reached the Mississippi River. They found that the great river flowed to the ocean.

La Salle and Frontenac devised a plan to claim the waterway for France. They would build forts at key sites along the river. This allowed the French to control the continent's fur trade. It would also block English and Spanish settlers from moving west.

the expedition of Father Jacques Marquette and Louis Joliet

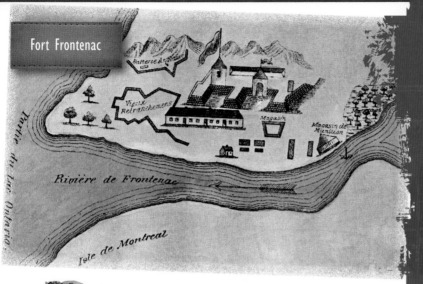

Fort Frontenac

La Salle suggested building the first fort on Lake Ontario near the Saint Lawrence River. The king of France made La Salle the leader of the new fort called *Fort Frontenac*. La Salle returned to New France to lead the fort's construction. The fort included farmland and a church. As the fort's leader, La Salle became one of the richest and most powerful men in New France.

Frontenac

Success Story

In 1673, Frontenac sent an expedition to find a water route to the West. It was led by a French priest named Jacques Marquette and a French fur trapper named Louis Joliet.

Marquette and Joliet followed waterways from Montreal to Lake Michigan. From there, they paddled up the Fox River and across Lake Winnebago (win-uh-BEY-goh). Within a month, they had found the Wisconsin River, which led them to the mighty Mississippi River. They discovered that the Mississippi flowed south all the way to the Gulf of Mexico. They had found a water route across North America to the ocean!

The Second Expedition
A New Adventure

La Salle's command of Fort Frontenac had made him rich and powerful. But what he really wanted was adventure. In 1677, he began planning a second expedition. This time, he wanted to explore the Mississippi River. He planned to claim more land for France.

La Salle traveled to France to get **permission** from King Louis XIV. The king met with many important people in France. They all said that La Salle was a smart man with good sense. So the king granted La Salle the right to explore the river and build forts along the way.

In 1678, La Salle returned to New France. He had the iron, sails, and ropes to build a ship for the journey. He also brought with him a crew of shipbuilders. A new friend came along, too. Henri de Tonti (AHN-ree day TAWN-tee) was a former Italian army officer. He would be La Salle's **second-in-command**.

La Salle asks King Louis XIV for permission to explore the Mississippi River.

Tonti supervised the building of the ship on the Niagara River near Lake Erie. The builders worked in cold conditions in the winter. In the summer of 1679, the ship was ready to take its first voyage. La Salle had named it the *Griffin*.

drawing of the *Griffin*

constructing the *Griffin*

What Is a Griffin?

A griffin is a mythological creature with the wings and head of an eagle and the body of a lion. Frontenac had an image of a griffin on his family **coat of arms**.

Magic Powers

The *Griffin* was built on the Niagara River using wood from local trees. The ship became the first commercial ship to sail Lake Erie. American Indians who saw the ship were amazed by its size and huge white sails. They suspected that the men who built and sailed such an amazing ship had magical powers.

Setting Sail

On August 7, 1679, La Salle launched his second expedition. His crew included Tonti, Nika, and a French missionary named Father Louis Hennepin (HEN-uh-pin). In the *Griffin*, they sailed the entire lengths of lakes Erie, Ontario, and Huron (YOOR-uhn). The ship reached Green Bay on the west side of Lake Michigan in September.

At Green Bay, the crew met a group of La Salle's traders. These men had furs to sell in Montreal. La Salle needed money to pay off his debts. So he sent the men and the furs home in the *Griffin*. He told them to rejoin the expedition as soon as possible.

La Salle at Niagara Falls

La Salle and 14 men continued their journey by canoe. They paddled the length of Lake Michigan, braving violent storms. Finally, they reached the Saint Joseph River at the southern end of the lake. They built a **primitive** log fort. They called it Fort Saint Joseph.

During this time, La Salle realized that the *Griffin* was never coming back. Some people thought it sank in a storm. Others suspected the crew of stealing the furs and sinking the ship. To this day, no trace of the *Griffin*, its cargo, or the crew has ever been found.

Father Hennepin riding in a canoe.

Travel Log

Father Louis Hennepin was a Catholic missionary. Like La Salle, he longed for adventure and the glory of new discoveries. He went on La Salle's second expedition and later wrote a book about the journey. He was the first European to write about Niagara Falls.

Extreme Paddling

Even today, Lake Michigan is known for its unpredictable weather. Paddling across its waters is dangerous. La Salle and his crew were blown around by high winds and beached by crashing waves. They slept on the cold ground on the shore and looked for pumpkins and corn to eat.

More Bad Luck

During the winter of 1679, La Salle and his men pushed on in search of the Mississippi River. They paddled up the Saint Joseph River. They carried their canoes five miles (8 km) to the Kankakee (kang-kuh-KEE) River. From there, they paddled into the Illinois River.

La Salle's crew was cold, tired, and miserable. As they paddled down the Illinois River, they came upon an American Indian village. The tribe welcomed the men with a feast and gave them shelter.

La Salle and his men receive food and shelter from Illinois American Indians.

Fort Crèvecoeur

Several days later, La Salle found that six of his men had **deserted** the expedition. This, along with the winter weather, brought the trip to a halt. The men began building a fort. La Salle called it *Fort Crèvecoeur* (krev-KEUR), the French word for "brokenhearted."

In the spring, La Salle divided the men into three groups. Father Hennepin led one group in search of the Mississippi River. Tonti stayed at the fort with another group to build a new ship. La Salle, Nika, and four others headed back to Fort Frontenac for supplies.

La Salle and his men endured another trek through ice and snow. Meanwhile, there was a **mutiny** at Fort Crèvecoeur. And Father Hennepin was captured by American Indians!

Close Call

Not only did many of La Salle's men desert him, but one of them may also have tried to kill him! According to Tonti, someone poisoned La Salle's food. He nearly died. Luckily, he had medicine from France that saved his life.

Safety First

Fort Crèvecoeur was built to protect the Frenchmen. Its walls were made of 12-inch (30 cm) thick wood. They were buried three feet (91 cm) in the ground and stood 25 feet (8 m) high. Inside, there was a **forge**. A forge is a workshop for making metal tools and weapons. There was also a **stockpile** of weapons and ammunition.

Success at Last

In 1681, La Salle set out again for the Mississippi River. The expedition reached the Mississippi in February. As they paddled south, the weather got warmer. Food was plentiful, and the men were in good spirits. They made friends with American Indian tribes. And they saw new animals, including alligators!

In April 1682, La Salle finally reached the Gulf of Mexico. He claimed the region for France. He named it *Louisiana* (loo-ee-zee-AN-uh) in honor of King Louis XIV. But La Salle returned to New France to find himself at odds with the new governor. He sailed to France to get help from the king.

La Salle claims Louisiana for France.

King Louis XIV

Problems at Home

New France's new governor took La Salle's property and put someone else in charge of the forts La Salle had built. La Salle asked King Louis XIV for help. The king gave control of the forts back to La Salle and made him governor of the new Louisiana Territory.

Gold and Greed

It was well-known that the Spanish had found gold and silver in Mexico. King Louis XIV wanted these riches for himself. The fort in the Gulf would be near Mexico, which was Spanish territory. From there, the French could take over the Spanish gold and silver mines.

In November, France was about to go to war with Spain. King Louis XIV was pleased when La Salle arrived with news that he had claimed the Mississippi River. He liked La Salle's plan to build a fort at the mouth of the river and to build French settlements along the river. He also liked the idea of forming **alliances** with the local American Indians to fight the Spanish. Louis XIV sent La Salle back to New France with four ships, around 150 soldiers, and many settlers.

Landing in Texas

In the summer of 1684, La Salle led his fifth expedition. Four ships sailed from France to the Gulf of Mexico. They spent weeks searching for the Mississippi River. La Salle sent some men to explore the Texas coast at Cedar Bayou. In February 1685, the ships entered Matagorda (mah-tah-GOHR-dah) Bay on the coast of Texas. But they had missed the river by 500 miles (805 km).

La Salle's crew of around 200 people had a hard time in Texas. The Spanish had taken one of La Salle's ships, and another sank. Most of the food, tools, and weapons sank with it.

La Salle's expedition exploring the Gulf of Mexico

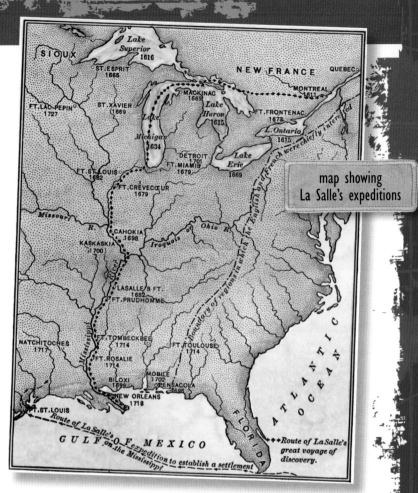

map showing La Salle's expeditions

Where Was Tonti?

Tonti was not on La Salle's final expedition. He led his own expedition to Matagorda Bay three years later. But he did not find any survivors at the Matagorda Bay settlement.

Fort Saint Louis?

People have long called the fort that La Salle built in Texas *Fort Saint Louis*. But historians have recently discovered that La Salle and his men never used this name for their fort. The name was given to the fort long after the settlement had disappeared.

The miserable crew camped on the swampy shore between the present-day cities of Galveston and Corpus Christi. Spoiled food and **brackish** (BRAK-ish), or salty, water made the people sick. They also had to deal with **hostile** American Indians in the area. Many people in the group died in the first two years of the settlement. To make matters worse, the following year, their only remaining ship, *La Belle*, was destroyed during a storm!

Tragic Ending

La Salle spent most of 1685 and 1686 away from his Texas fort. He was busy exploring Texas and searching for the Mississippi River. On one expedition, La Salle travelled east and met the Tejas and Caddo American Indians. He learned that the Mississippi was to his east. He made plans to find it.

In January 1687, La Salle and 20 men began their journey to find the mighty river. He left women, children, and disabled people at the fort. Local Karankawa American Indians attacked and destroyed the fort. They killed all of the adults and adopted the children.

La Salle and his men meet with a group of Caddo.

Many of La Salle's men disliked him. After a fight, two of La Salle's men planned to kill him. The next day, Pierre Duhaut (doo-HOH) shot and killed La Salle. La Salle was 43 years old.

La Salle's life ended in tragedy, but his legacy lives on. His alliances with American Indians helped the French survive in North America. Many people credit La Salle with the European settlement of Texas and the American Southwest.

La Salle is shot.

The Talons

Lucien and Isabelle Talon and their children were among La Salle's crew in Texas. Isabelle gave birth to a sixth child during the expedition. While in Texas, Lucien disappeared in the woods and was never heard from again.

Pierre, the oldest Talon son, joined La Salle on his last journey. After La Salle was killed, Pierre was adopted by a group of Caddo. When a group of Karankawa raided the camp, the American Indian attackers took the Talon children. When the children were rescued three years later, they had American Indian tattoos on their bodies and faces.

Archaeologists dig up the remains of *La Belle*.

Digging Up Texas History

In 1687, the last ship of La Salle's expedition, *La Belle*, was wrecked in a storm. It sank to the bottom of the shallow Matagorda Bay off the Texas coast. Almost 300 years later, **archaeologists** (ahr-kee-OL-uh-justs) decided to look for the sunken ship. Archaeologists are people who study items and people from the past. They try to learn about how people used to live.

The archaeologists used special tools to find metal and other objects on the floor of the bay. They found several shipwrecks, but not *La Belle*. Finally, in 1995, they decided to make one last attempt to find La Salle's ship—and they found it!

At first, they were not sure if it was *La Belle*. There have been many shipwrecks off the Texas coast. Then, they found musket balls. These are bullets from guns over 150 years old. They also found a large cannon with the crest of King Louis XIV on it. After putting the evidence together, they realized they had finally found *La Belle*!

Watery Grave

Archaeologists did not expect to find much left of the shipwreck. Wood usually rots under water. But researchers realized that mud had covered and **preserved** the boat. They even found barrels whose contents were still the way La Salle's crew had loaded them!

Cofferdam

Since *La Belle* was buried under water, archaeologists built walls and a dam around the sunken ship. This construction, which is called a *cofferdam*, kept the water out of their dig site. Over the next eight months, archaeologists dug up the remains of *La Belle* to learn more about the La Salle Expedition.

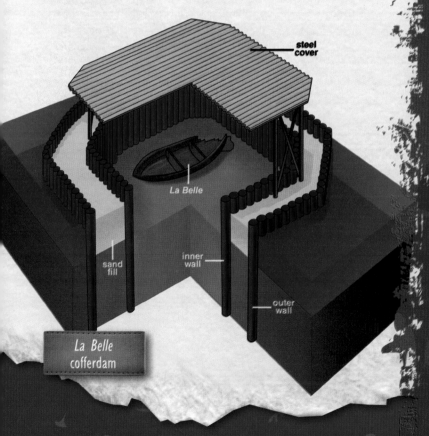

steel cover

La Belle

sand fill

inner wall

outer wall

La Belle cofferdam

Glossary

alliances—associations of groups who agree to cooperate for common goals

archaeologists—scientists who study ancient people and cultures

brackish—salty

captive—a person held against his or her will; a prisoner

coat of arms—a design, usually on a shield, that is unique to a particular family

deserted—left without permission

eddies—movements in rivers in which the current doubles back and forms whirls

expeditions—trips made for a specific purpose, especially to explore

foraged—searched for food

forge—a workshop for making objects out of metal

hostile—very unfriendly

Jesuit—a Roman Catholic religious order devoted to missionary work and education

missionaries—people who share their religious faith with others, usually in other countries

moccasins—soft leather shoes without heels

mutiny—a rebellion against legal authority

outpost—a settlement on a frontier or in a faraway place

pelts—the skin of an animal with the fur still attached

permission—agreement to allow something

portaging—carrying boats overland

preserved—protected or kept safe

primitive—very simple in design

remote—far from civilization or populated areas

revival—new interest or coming back to life

second-in-command—a person ranking below the person in command

seminary—a school for the training of priests

stockpile—an extra supply of something for use during a time of shortage

trading post—a store in a remote location where traders barter, or trade, for supplies

trinkets—small items of little value